CHILD
DEVELOPMENT

Throughout the book we have referred to the child as "he" or "him" – obviously we do so only for convenience. Similarly, we often refer to the "parent" – by which we mean either the mother or father or any other person who may be acting, either temporarily or permanently, in a parental role.

Acknowledgment
The Diagram Group would like to thank the following specialists in child development whose detailed research provided the basis for much of the information presented in this book: L. B. Ames, A. Gessell, R. Griffiths, F. L. Ilg, R. S. Illingworth, M. Sheridan.

CHILD DEVELOPMENT

A Comprehensive Guide to Your Child's Growth and Ability

The Diagram Group

CORGI BOOKS

CHILD DEVELOPMENT

A CORGI BOOK 0552 12741 8

First publication in Great Britain

PRINTING HISTORY

Corgi edition published 1986

This book is set in 9/11pt Baskerville

Corgi Books are published by Transworld Publishers Ltd.,
61–63 Uxbridge Road, Ealing, London W5 5SA, in Australia
by Transworld Publishers (Aust.) Pty. Ltd., 26 Harley
Crescent, Condell Park, NSW 2200, and in New Zealand by
Transworld Publishers (N.Z.) Ltd., Cnr. Moselle and
Waipareira Avenues, Henderson, Auckland.

Printed and bound in Great Britain by
Cox & Wyman Ltd, Reading

Foreword

Children, like marrows, come in all sizes from the very large to the very small. Unfortunately their development is more complicated than that of marrows, since no marrows are born geniuses and none a little slow on the uptake. By and large, however, most babies end up ordinary citizens like you and me. Strictly speaking, there is no such thing as a normal child – only an average one. So unless you are seriously concerned about an aspect of your offspring's development which is manifestly retarded – take heart! Some children walk early and talk late and some, out of sheer perversity, do the opposite. But in the end it is very likely that your child will soon catch up with that gifted girl who talked at six months, or that brilliant boy who seems destined to be an Olympic champion. This book is written to help you decide whether or not you need be concerned about your child's progress. Remember that it is a reference book. It should not be read from cover to cover at one sitting like a novel, nor should it be regarded as an infallible Bible. Sensibly used, however, it should save you enough worry to let you enjoy your children's growing years. If so, it will have achieved its purpose.

Dr. Geoffrey Smerdon
M.A .(Oxon), B.M., B.Ch., M.F.O.M.(R.C.P.)

CONTENTS

Section 1
PHYSICAL DEVELOPMENT

Introduction

This first section describes the physical development of boys
and girls from birth to the end of puberty. Height more than
triples in children of both sexes while weight typically increases
by about 16 times in girls and 19 times in boys. Growth brings
significant changes in body proportions – with the head coming
to account for progressively less, and the legs for more, of the
total height. Other physical developments include the fusing
together of more than 100 bones in the body and the
replacement of a child's primary teeth by adult ones. Perhaps
the most dramatic changes of all, however, occur during
puberty – when the body of a child is transformed by sexual
maturation into the body of an adult.

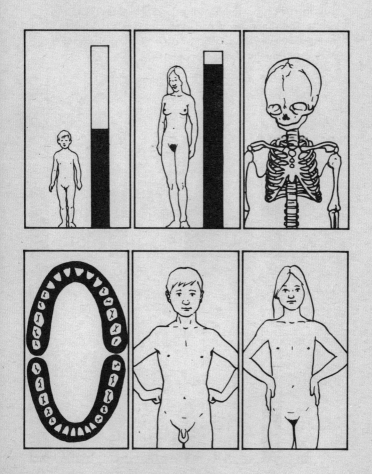

height

The illustrations here and overleaf show typical patterns of growth for boys and girls from birth until they reach adult height during their teens.

During the first three years, growth is rapid for children of both sexes, but successive measurements during this period show that the rate of growth is slowing down. Heights of boys and girls typically increase by half as much again from birth to 12 months, but even this rate of growth is slower than during the three months immediately before birth.

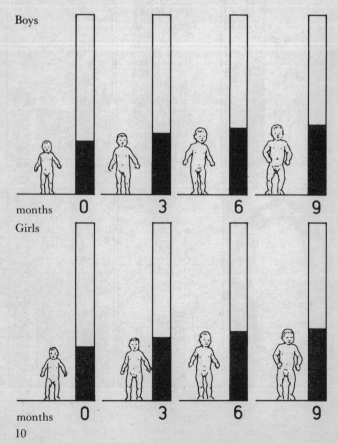

Boys

months   0   3   6   9

Girls

months   0   3   6   9

Age	Boys	Girls
0 months	19.9in (50.5cm)	19.8in (50.3cm)
3 months	23.8in (60.4cm)	23.4in (59.4cm)
6 months	26.1in (66.3cm)	25.7in (65.3cm)
9 months	28.0in (71.1cm)	27.6in (70.1cm)
12 months	29.6in (75.2cm)	29.2in (74.1cm)
18 months	32.2in (81.8cm)	31.8in (80.8cm)
2 years	34.4in (87.4cm)	34.1in (86.6cm)
3 years	37.9in (96.3cm)	37.7in (95.8cm)

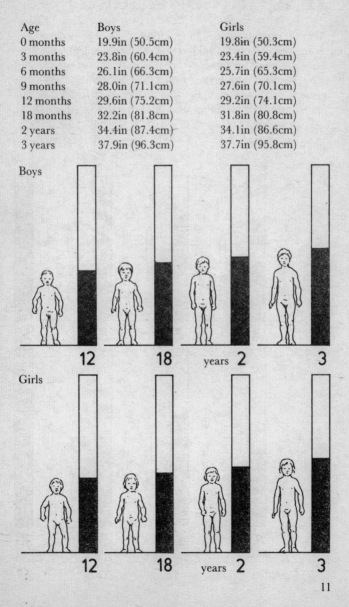

Boys

12   18   years 2   3

Girls

12   18   years 2   3

height (continued)

After the rapid growth of the first three years, height increases more slowly in middle childhood. The onset of puberty is linked to a sharp spurt in growth that peaks just before the beginning of adolescence: Girls mature earlier than boys, and usually stop growing by about age 16. In males the growth spurt is later, and growth often continues after 18.

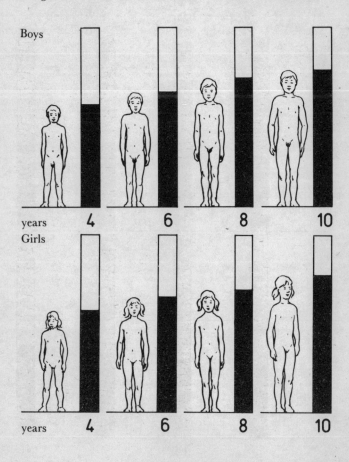

Boys

years 4 6 8 10

Girls

years 4 6 8 10

Age	Boys	Girls
4 years	40.7in (1.033m)	40.6in (1.031m)
6 years	46.3in (1.176m)	45.6in (1.158m)
8 years	51.2in (1.30m)	50.4in (1.28m)
10 years	55.2in (1.40m)	54.6in (1.39m)
12 years	58.9in (1.50m)	59.8in (1.52m)
14 years	64.0in (1.63m)	62.8in (1.60m)
16 years	67.8in (1.72m)	63.9in (1.62m)
18 years	68.9in (1.75m)	63.9in (1.62m)

Boys

12   14   16   18

Girls

12   14   16   18

weight

Average patterns of weight gain broadly follow those for
increasing height. There is a rapid but slowing weight increase
during the first three years (with major differences in
birthweights tending to be largely averaged out in the first six
months), a period of slower weight increase during middle
childhood, and then major weight gains associated with the
onset of puberty (with girls gaining most between 10 and 14
years and boys between 12 and 16 years).

Age	Boys	Girls
0 months	7.5lb (3.40kg)	7.4lb (3.35kg)
3 months	12.6lb (5.55kg)	12.4lb (5.46kg)
6 months	16.7lb (7.58kg)	16.0lb (7.26kg)
9 months	20.0lb (9.07kg)	19.2lb (8.70kg)
10 months	22.2lb (10.06kg)	21.5lb (9.75kg)
18 months	25.2lb (11.43kg)	24.5lb (11.11kg)
2 years	27.7lb (12.56kg)	27.1lb (12.29kg)
3 years	32.2lb (14.61kg)	31.8lb (14.43kg)
4 years	36.4lb (16.5kg)	36.2lb (16.3kg)
6 years	48.3lb (21.9kg)	46.5lb (21.1kg)
8 years	60.1lb (27.3kg)	58.1lb (26.4kg)
10 years	71.9lb (32.6kg)	70.3lb (31.9kg)
12 years	84.4lb (38.3kg)	87.6lb (39.7kg)
14 years	107.6lb (48.8kg)	108.4lb (49.2kg)
16 years	129.7lb (58.8kg)	117.0lb (53.1kg)
18 years	143.0lb (64.9kg)	120.0lb (54.4kg)

heights and weights compared

These diagrams show the average heights (**1**) and weights (**2**)
of boys and girls at different ages. Boys are generally taller and
heavier than girls of the same age, except when the earlier onset
of puberty in girls causes them to spurt ahead for a time in
terms of both height and weight.

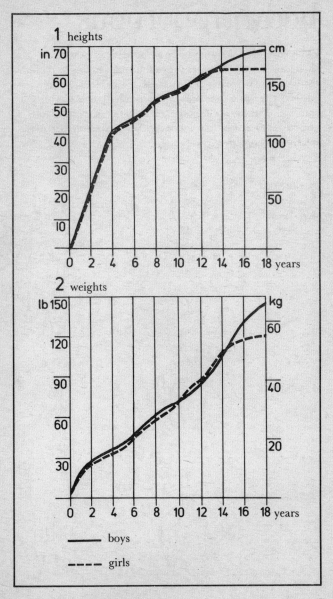

1 heights

2 weights

boys

girls

15

body proportions

From birth to adolescence body proportions are altered by changes in the growth rates of head, trunk, and limbs. While the head is one-quarter of the total length at birth it is only one-sixth by age six and one-eighth by adulthood. The legs start at only three-eights of the total length but increase to one-half of total length by maturity. The trunk becomes relatively slimmer.

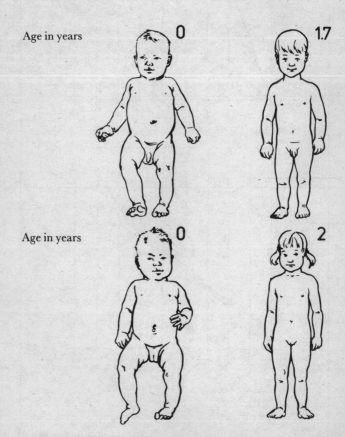

Age in years   **0**   **1.7**

Age in years   **0**   **2**

Changes in growth patterns for bone, muscle, and fat transform the chubby, short-limbed, relatively large-headed baby into the thinner, wiry schoolchild. Later, children broaden out – boys especially at the shoulders, girls at the hips. But eventual physique varies with individuals and may be detected early on, in some cases by the age of two.

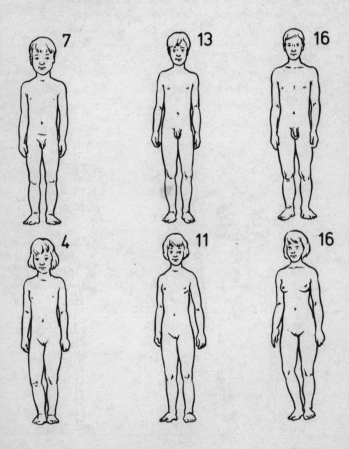

skeletal growth

The human skeleton develops gradually from connective tissues that become first cartilage and then bone. In fact, at birth, some 'bones' are still cartilage, and the process does not complete itself until about age 25. At the same time, many bones fuse together, so that the 330 in a baby's skeleton become 206 bones in an adult. Proportions also change. A newborn baby has a short neck, high shoulders, and a round chest. Between ages three and 10 the shoulders lower, the neck lengthens, and the chest broadens and flattens. Posture changes too: bow legs and knock knees, for example, are common to age five.

Skeletal differences between a newborn male (**1**) and an adult male (**2**).

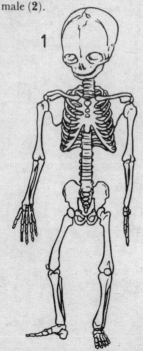
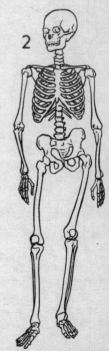

growth of body parts

Different parts of the body have different types of growth. This graph shows the percentage increase for each type from birth to adulthood.

1) General type (affecting most of the body including muscles, lungs, blood volume, intestines) spurts in infancy, slows in childhood, spurts towards adolescence, then decelerates.

2) Neural type (affecting brain, eyes, skull, spinal cord) spurts dramatically from birth to six years. By then 90% of neural growth is over.

3) Genital type (testes, ovaries, etc) stays minimal, then spurts at puberty and during adolescence.

4) Lymphoid type (thymus and lymph nodes) peaks from 10 to 12 years, then lymph and thymus tissue shrinks. Hence the graph shows lymphoid type reaching 200% before diminishing.

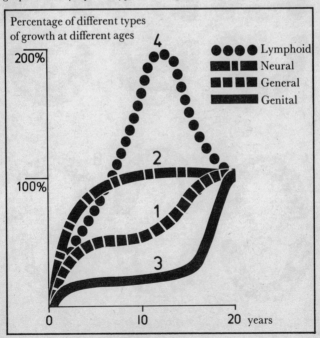

Percentage of different types of growth at different ages

●●●● Lymphoid
■■■ Neural
■■■ General
■■ Genital

200%

100%

0   10   20   years

teeth

The order in which the teeth appear – with typical ages for their appearance – is shown here in a series of diagrams.

Primary teeth The full primary set is made up of 20 teeth: eight incisors, four canines, and eight molars.

1) Lower central incisors, 6–8 months
2) Upper central incisors, 7–9 months
3) Lateral incisors, 9–13 months
4) First molars, 12–15 months
5) Canines, 16–18 months
6) Second molars, 20–30 months

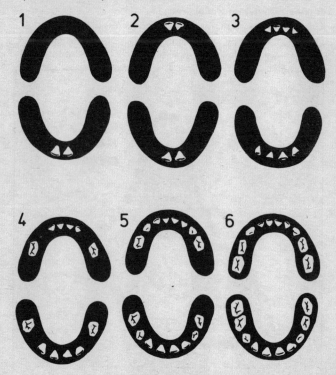

Adult teeth There are 32 teeth in the full adult set: eight incisors, four canines, eight premolars, and 12 molars.

1) First molars, 6–7 years
2) Central incisors, 7–8 years
3) Lateral incisors, 8–9 years
4) First premolars, 10–12 years
5) Second premolars, 10–12 years
6) Canines, 12–14 years
7) Second molars, 12–16 years
8) Third molars (wisdom teeth), 17–25 years

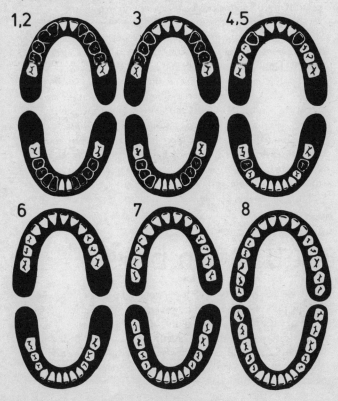

changes at puberty

The physical changes of puberty transform the body of a child into that of an adult. These changes take place over a number of years, and occur in response to the production of sex hormones (testosterone in the male and estrogen in the female). The age at which puberty occurs varies, but in general it starts and finishes earlier in girls than in boys.

The most significant development of puberty is the maturing of the sex organs. Girls begin to menstruate and, after the first few periods, begin to produce mature ova (eggs) during the menstrual cycle. In males, maturing of the sex organs during puberty results in the production of sperm, which are sometimes emitted from the penis during sleep.

Male and female hormones are also responsible for the development during puberty of what are called secondary sexual characteristics. Before puberty, except for very obvious genital differences, the physical appearance of boys and girls is fairly similar. During puberty, differences between the two sexes are emphasized. Girls generally do not grow as tall as boys. Girls develop rounded contours and broad hips, compared with the angular, more muscular male physique. Both sexes develop coarse body hair during puberty but it occurs in different areas and is heavier in males. Also at this time, a boy's larynx grows more than a girl's, making his Adam's apple more pronounced and his voice deeper.

puberty in boys

Here we describe a typical developmental pattern for a boy during puberty. There are, however, considerable and perfectly normal variations between individuals.

Before puberty (**1**), the penis and scrotum are small, and there is no pubic, underarm, or other coarse body hair. In early puberty (**2**) – perhaps from 12 to 15 – the testes begin to enlarge, pubic hair appears at the base of the penis, the penis begins to grow, and there is a sudden, rapid increase in height. As puberty continues (**3**) – perhaps from 15 to 18 – the shoulders broaden, the voice deepens, hair grows in the armpits and on the upper lip, penis growth continues, sperm are produced, pubic hair coarsens and spreads, other body hair grows, the prostate gland enlarges, height and weight increase, and there is a sudden increase in strength.

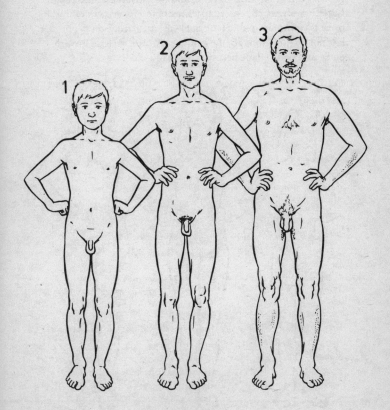

puberty in girls

This is a typical developmental pattern for a girl during puberty, but as with boys there are considerable normal variations.

Before puberty (**1**), the breasts are undeveloped, there is no pubic or underarm hair, and the body shape is boyish. In early puberty (**2**) – perhaps from age 11 to 13 – the face becomes fuller, the pelvis widens, fat is deposited on the hips, the breasts start to develop and the nipples stand out, pubic hair begins to grow, the vaginal walls thicken, and menstruation may begin. Later in puberty (**3**) – perhaps from 14 to 17 – growth of the breasts continues, pubic hair thickens, menstruation begins if it has not already done so, the genitals mature, skeletal growth ends, and body shape becomes more rounded.

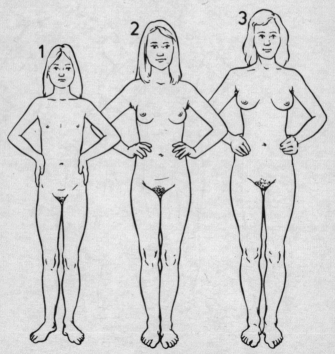

The onset of menstruation Some girls start to menstruate as early as nine, whereas others may be 16 or 17. Most begin between the ages of 12 and 14. A medical examination is needed if the first period has not occurred by age 18. Menstruation is the outward sign of the routine cycle of hormone change and ovum production that occurs in females from puberty to the menopause. During the first part of each cycle the lining of the uterus (womb) swells with blood and tissue in preparation for receiving a fertilized ovum. If the ovum remains unfertilized after ovulation (release of an ovum), all but the deepest layers of the uterine lining are discharged, with the ovum, as the menstrual flow. The monthly cycle then repeats itself.

A typical cycle – as shown in the diagram below – lasts 28 days, but there are variations from woman to woman, and sometimes from month to month. Adolescents in particular are prone to irregular periods.

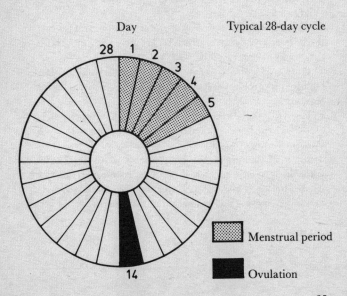

Day

Typical 28-day cycle

Menstrual period

Ovulation

Section 2
MOTOR DEVELOPMENT

Introduction

After a description of the 'primitive' reflex actions of newborn babies, this section goes on to describe typical stages passed through as a young child gains mastery over his limbs and learns to sit, crawl, stand, and walk. The stages described in this book – and especially the ages at which they are shown to occur – provide no more than a very general guide: exact patterns of motor development vary quite normally from one child to another.

General trends An overview of motor development reveals three broad trends, all of which reflect increasing maturation of the child's nervous system.

1) Outward: central body areas function before outer areas. Children control upper legs and upper arms earlier than lower legs, forearms, and hands.

2) Head to foot: head control comes before hauling the body along with the hands. Creeping on hands and knees follows. Walking comes last of all.

3) Big to small muscles: early movements are wild jerks of the whole body, trunk, or entire limbs. Control of small muscles is needed before a child can pick up a crumb with thumb and forefinger, and walk with an economical action.

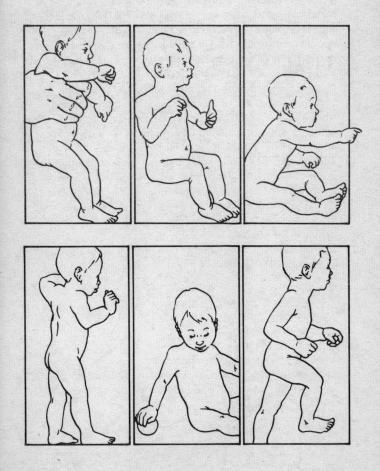

reflexes of the newborn

A variety of reflexes – automatic reactions to particular changes in surroundings – are present in a newborn baby. Known as 'primitive' reflexes, they are thought to be a legacy from man's earliest ancestors, when such actions were vital for an infant's survival. Testing them soon after a baby's birth provides doctors with an indication of the baby's general condition and the normality of his central nervous system. (Parents are warned not to rest some of these reflexes for themselves.)

By three months a baby's primitive reflexes have generally been replaced by voluntary movements. This can only happen when a baby learns to associate a particular action with the fulfilment of a certain need; he learns, for instance, that hunger is satisfied by food, which is obtained by sucking.

1) Rooting reflex If one side of a baby's cheek or mouth is gently touched, he will turn his head in the direction of the touch. This ensures that he will seek out the nipple when his cheek is brushed by his mother's breast. With the sucking and swallowing reflexes, the rooting reflex is essential for successful feeding in the newborn.

2) Blink reflex A baby blinks in response to various stimuli – for instance, if the bridge of his nose is touched.

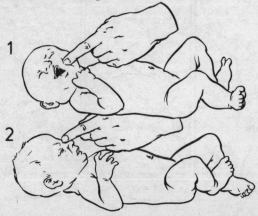

3) Doll's eye reflex If a baby's head is turned to the left or right, there is a delay in the following of the eyes.

4) Asymmetric tonic neck reflex When on his back and not crying, a newborn baby lies with his head to one side, the arm on that side extended and the opposite leg bent at the knee.

5) Grasp reflex This reflex makes a baby automatically clench his fist if an object is placed in his palm. If a finger is slipped into each of his palms, a baby will grasp them so tightly that he can support his own weight. The grasp reflex can also be evoked from the toes.

6) Moro reflex This reflex is seen when the baby is startled. The arms and legs are outstretched and then drawn inward with the fingers curled as if ready to clutch at something. A baby's Moro reflex is tested to check muscle tone; if the limbs respond asymmetrically, there may be a weakness or injury of a particular limb.

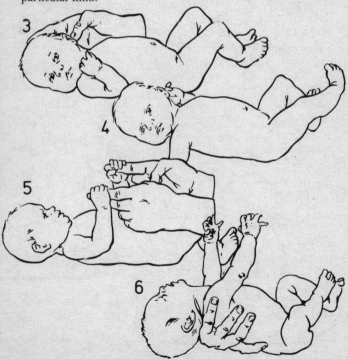

reflexes of the newborn (continued)

7) Crossed extension reflex If one of the baby's legs is held in an extended position and the sole of that foot stroked, the other leg flexes, draws towards the body, and then extends.

8) 'Walking' reflex If a baby is held upright with the soles of his feet on a flat surface, and is then moved forward slowly, he will respond with 'walking' steps.

9) 'Stepping' reflex If the front of his leg is gently brought into contact with the edge of a table, a baby will raise his leg and take a 'step' up on to the table.

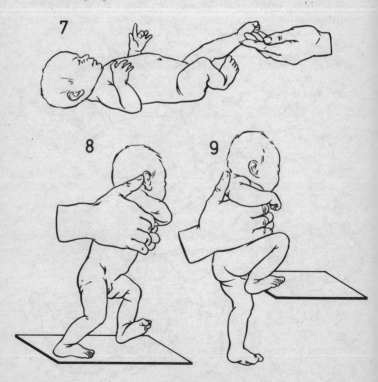

secondary responses

So-called secondary responses begin appearing at about four months when primitive reflexes decline. Some secondary responses may be absent in normal babies before one year. Vital in later life, secondary responses concern balancing, rolling, and protection of the falling body.

1) Downward parachute If someone holds a baby upright then swiftly lowers him, the legs stretch and move apart as though anticipating a hard landing.

2) Forward parachute If someone holds a baby upright (**a**) and swiftly tilts him forward towards the ground, arms and fingers outstretch and spread protectively (**b**).

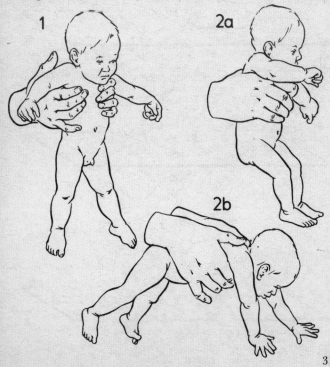

secondary responses (continued)

3) Rolling response From the fourth month, rolling the body over by the legs (**a**) evokes a complex response involving the baby's head and unimpeded arm (**b**).

4) Sideways propping reaction This time a child sitting upright is tilted sideways. He extends an arm and hand, pressing on the ground to stop his body falling.

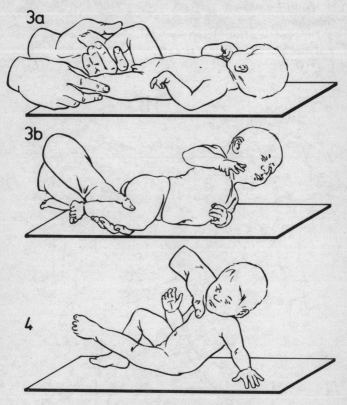

3a

3b

4

baby held horizontally

These three illustrations show the increasing capabilities of a baby held in a horizontal position.

1) A newborn baby's head droops – he lacks the coordination and strength required to raise it.

2) At six weeks he can raise his head in line with his body, but can do so only for a minute.

3) By 12 weeks he can lift his head well above the general body line and hold it there for a time.

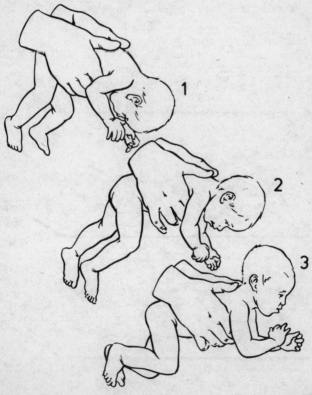

crawling

Here and on subsequent pages are typical stages in learning to crawl as a preliminary to walking.

1) Placed in a prone position, the newborn baby draws his knees up beneath his abdomen and lies with his pelvis high and his head directed to one side.

2) By six weeks old he tends to lie less tucked up. His pelvis is lower. His legs are more extended and he sometimes kicks out. Now and then he lifts his chin well up.

3) By 12 weeks the baby lies with legs fully extended and pelvis flat upon the bed or couch. He raises his chin and shoulders and may hold his head almost upright.

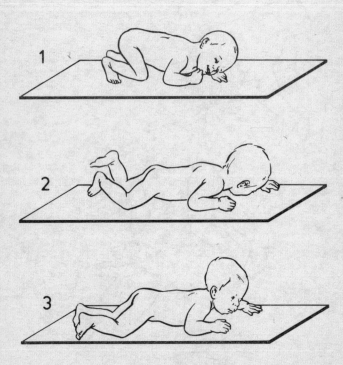

4) At 16 weeks he can press down with his forearms to lift his head and the front part of his chest. He also stretches all his limbs, and 'swims' on his abdomen.

5) By 20 weeks the infant has had some weeks of practice and uses his forearms in an even surer manner than before to help him lift up his head and upper chest.

6) By 24 weeks he can lift his entire head, chest, and upper abdomen. Thrusting down with outstretched arms, he bears the weight of his upper body on his hands.

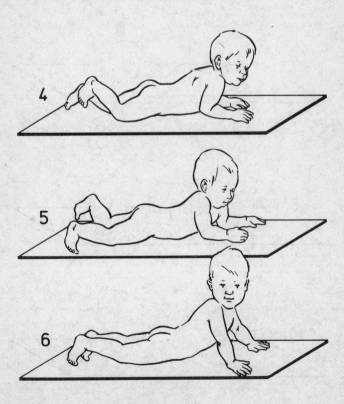

crawling (continued)

7) By 28 weeks the bay lies with the upper part of his body supported only on one hand. (By this time he is also able to roll over from abdomen to back and vice versa.)

8) The 36-week-old infant learns that by thrusting down and forward on a surface he can move his body backwards. He is well on the way to true crawling.

9) At 40 weeks he crawls forward on his belly, pulling himself along with his hands. At this stage his legs do no more than trail along the ground.

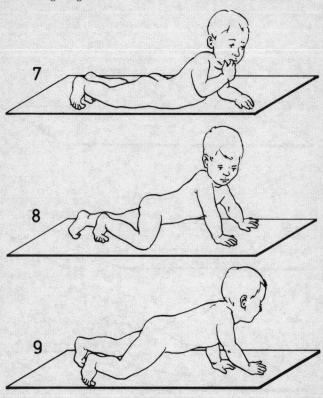

10) By 44 weeks he has learned a more agile mode of crawling. Arms and legs all work together as he now creeps along on hands and knees, with belly on the ground.

11) At one year old he rests some weight upon his soles and ambles bear-like on his hands and feet. He has reached the final stage before unaided walking.

12) At 15 months he sometimes still feels safest on all fours, for instance when he starts tackling that formidable stepped cliff known to adults as a staircase.

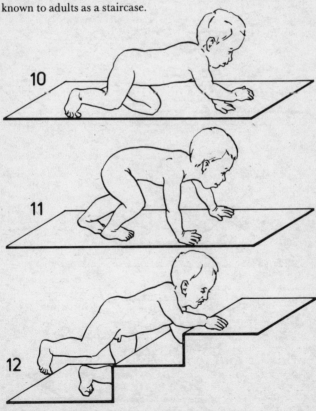

sitting

Described next are stages by which a baby learns to sit.

1) The newborn baby cannot sit, and his head lags flaccidly if he is pulled into a sitting position.

2) At four weeks his head still lags but lifts briefly if he is held to sit. His back is rounded.

3) By 12 weeks a baby supported to sit holds his head up, but the head may still bob forward.

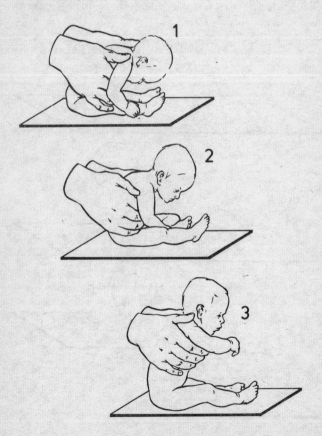

4) At 16 weeks only the lower back of the supported baby is curved. The head wobbles if the body sways.

5) By 20 weeks there is no head lag or wobble and the baby pulled to sit keeps his back straight.

6) At 24 weeks he lifts his head to be pulled up, and sits supported in a high chair or baby carriage.

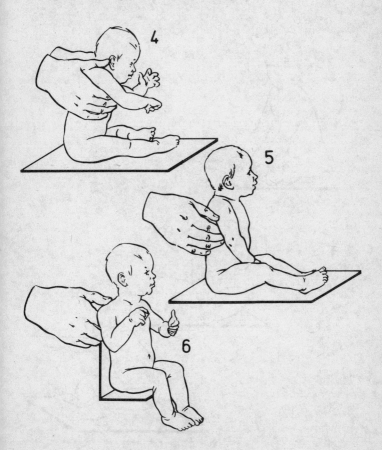

sitting (continued)

7) At 28 weeks a baby can sit alone on the floor, but uses arms and hands as props for his unsteady body.
8) By 32 weeks he is already able to sit on the floor, briefly unsupported by his arms.
9) At 36 weeks he can sit for 10 minutes, regaining balance if he bends his body forward.

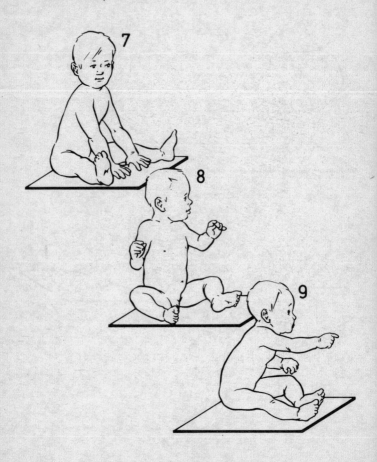

10) By 40 weeks the sitting child can lie down on his stomach and return to a sitting position.
11) By 48 weeks the sitting child can twist around to pick up something, yet keep his balance.
12) About 15 months he sits down in a low chair, climbing forward into it and then turning around.

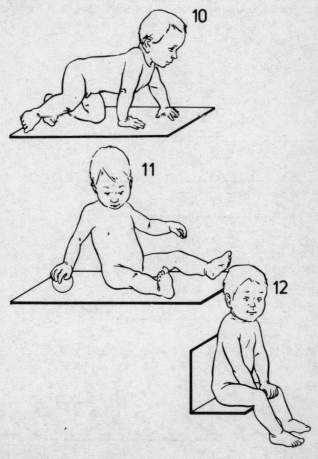

standing and walking

Typical stages by which a child learns to stand, then walk, and then extend his motor capabilities are given below and on the next five pages.
1) A newborn baby held with the sole of his foot on a table moves his legs in a reflex walking action (also see pp. 30–31).
2) At eight weeks the baby briefly keeps his head up if he is held in a standing position.

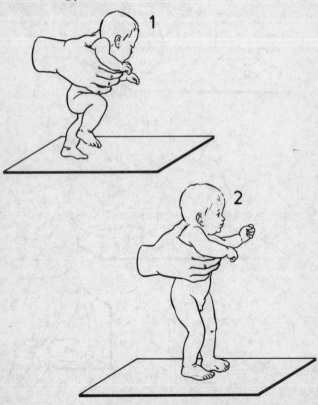

3) By 36 weeks he can pull himself up and remains standing by grasping hold of furniture.
4) By 48 weeks he can walk forward if both hands are held (or sideways, gripping furniture).

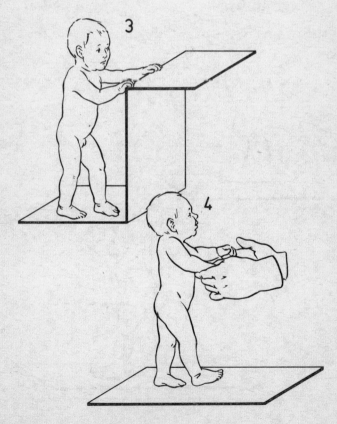

standing and walking (continued)

5) At one year the child walks forward if someone holds one of his hands.
6) By 13 months he has become capable of walking without help.

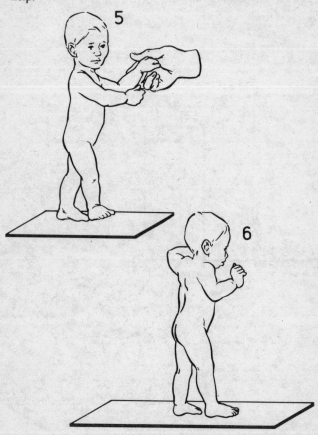

7) At 18 months he can go up and down stairs without assistance.
8) By two he runs, walks backward, and picks things up without overbalancing.

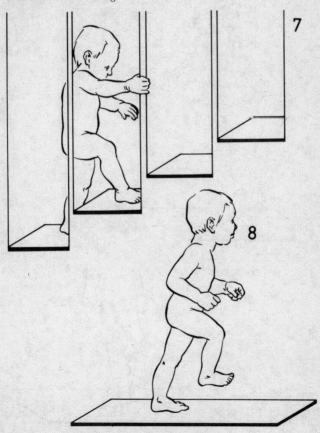

standing and walking (continued)

9) At 2½ the child can balance on tiptoe, and jump with both feet.

10) At three he can balance for some seconds while standing on one foot.

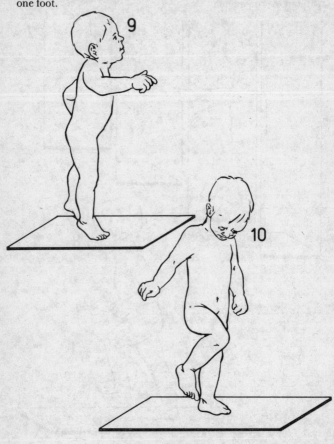

11) At four he walks down stairs by placing only one foot on each step.

12) At five he skips on both feet.

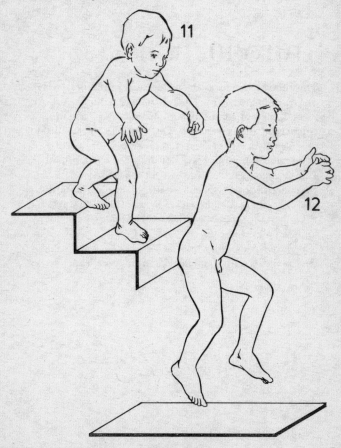

Section 3
ASPECTS IN DEVELOPMENT

Introduction

This third section looks at a whole range of abilities developed during childhood – visual, manipulative, auditory, vocal, mental, conceptual, social, and emotional. As in the previous chapter, the stages and ages mentioned here are intended to provide only a very general picture. Precise patterns of development vary quite normally from one child to another. During childhood, the development of acquired abilities and characteristics depends on increasing biological maturity and also on learning. Children learn in many different ways, and the importance of play as a means of learning should not be underestimated (see pp. 68–75).

The section ends with a brief look at emotional and social developments during childhood and on through adolescence.

field of vision

At birth a baby's eyes move independently. At this early stage he finds it hard to fix on any object with his eyes.

Soon after birth (**1**) he can watch a dangling ball swung through a 45° arc – one-quarter of an adult's field of vision.

By six weeks (**2**) he moves his eyes to watch a ball through 90°. (This coincides with the development of binocular vision: visual fields now overlap so that most of the image formed on one retina duplicates most of the image on the other.)

By three months (**3**) he can watch a ball swung through 180° – the full adult field of vision.

This progress partly reflects the baby's increasing mastery of the six muscles attaching each eyeball to its socket.

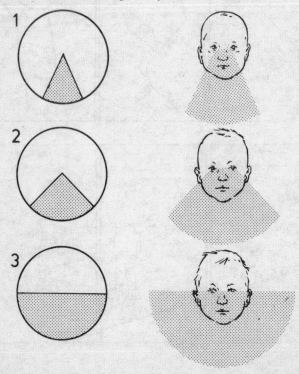

depth of vision

Depth of vision improves during the first year. A month-old baby gazes at a small white ball moved 6–10in (15–25cm) from his face, but not at one across the room. Tests with rolling balls of different diameters help to show the rate at which depth of vision improves. By six months old (**1**) a baby watches a ball ¼in (6mm) in diameter 10ft (3m) away. This suggests a visual acuity as measured by a standard eye-test card of 20/120: i.e. the baby can clearly focus an object 20ft away that someone with normal 20/20 vision would see clearly from 120ft away. By nine months (**2**) a baby watches a ball ⅛in (3mm) in diameter 10ft (3m) away, implying 20/60 vision. Such tests suggest 20/20 or normal visual acuity by one year old (**3**).

visual perception

Adults check their visual impressions against a memory bank stored in the brain. This helps instant recognition of the shapes, sizes, colours, positions, and other qualities of objects that are seen.

To the newborn infant with no experience to draw upon, the visible world may seem no more than a muddle of blotches. Perception dawns gradually. Tests devised by psychologists give an indication of the times at which visual perception of shape, size, and colour appear.

By six months old, tested infants could perceive simple forms. When one of three test blocks – a circle, triangle, and square – was sweetened, the infants learned to recognize and suck it.

At six months children reached for a small nearby rattle rather than a larger one farther away, although they appeared to be similar. (But a child is 10 years old before he can discount distance in a fully adult way to judge the size of an object.)

Colour vision dawns at about three months, when the cones in the eye's retina become sufficiently developed. Tested children of that age gazed longer at coloured paper than at grey paper of equal brightness.

manipulation

At birth the hands are closed; the reflex grasp action (pp. 28–29) is present. The hands are still closed at one month, but are often opened by two months. The grasp reflex has gone by three months and a baby can hold a rattle. At four months the hands meet in play. By six months he can deliberately, but awkwardly, grasp a cube (**1**). By this time he passes it from hand to hand and bangs it on a table. By eight months he begins to grip the cube with his thumb opposite his fingers (**2**). By nine months thumb and finger grip is good enough to pick up a sweet. By one year he holds a cube in a mature pincer grip of thumb and fingers (**3**). By two years he can turn a doorknob and unscrew lids. He is now clearly left- or right-handed. By 2½ he holds a pencil in his hand, no longer in his fist, and starts to scribble and draw.

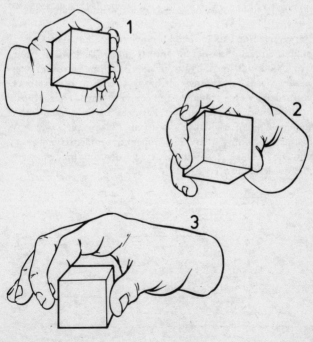

drawing

As hand-eye coordination and wrist control improves, children become capable of drawing an increasing number of shapes, always in the same sequence though sometimes earlier or later than the ages given here.

At two a child usually learns to copy a vertical line. At 2½ he can copy a horizontal line. At three he can copy a circle. By then he is also drawing a man, but shows no more than the head and maybe two other parts of the body (**1, 2**).

Only at age four does he manage to copy a cross by combining the vertical and horizontal strokes that he had mastered earlier. Another year may pass before he learns to rearrange these lines into a square. He can now draw a rather basic box-like type of house but quite likely cannot achieve the oblique strokes needed for showing a sloping roof. By five his man is more obviously human and may possess recognizable head, trunk, arms, and legs (**3**).

Between five and six the child becomes proficient at making oblique strokes and can now draw triangles. By seven he copies a diamond well, and fairly accurately inscribes a cross inside a square to make a 'window'. He has now built up a repertory of vertical, horizontal, oblique, and curved strokes. Thus armed, he draws increasingly complex houses and people, often with some touches of originality. For instance his people wear distinctive clothes (**4**) and may appear in profile. His house may have a smoking chimney and a garden containing flowers and bordered by a fence.

development of hearing

The hearing mechanism is fully formed at birth, but amniotic fluid in the eustachian tubes causes a few hours' deafness. Then a newborn baby begins to react to harsh, sharp sounds. By 10 days he responds to a loudly ticking watch or to a voice, and soon responds to sounds of different pitch and loudness. Sound localization improves over the first year. At three months a child turns his head vaguely towards a sound and his eyes seek it (**1**). At five months he turns his head, then inclines it, to locate a sound below ear level (**2**). At seven to eight months turning and inclination begin to merge (**3**). By nine to ten months the child swivels his head diagonally in a direct searching movement (**4**). By one year he localizes sound as well as any adult.

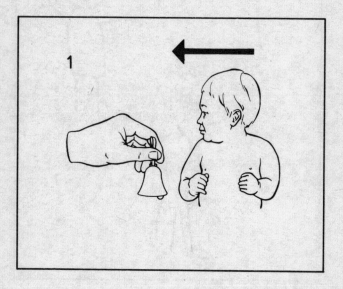

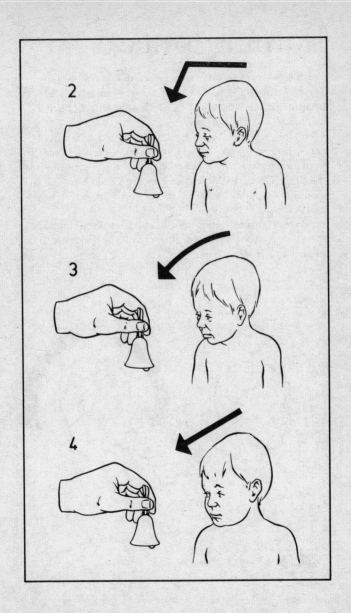

learning to speak

Learning to speak involves making and monitoring sounds.
Speech occurs when motor nerves bearing signals from the
brain operate the larynx and its vocal cords, also the pharynx,
soft palate, tongue, and lips.

Monitoring speech involves feedback to the brain. Sensory
nerves bring the brain signals from the speech muscles and
from the ears which have picked up sound waves pushed out by
the voice. Thanks to this feedback system a child learns to
modify the sounds he makes to match words that he has heard
others speaking.

It becomes markedly more difficult to learn to speak after age
three so it is important that deafness should be diagnosed and
treated as soon as possible.

Speech   Feedback

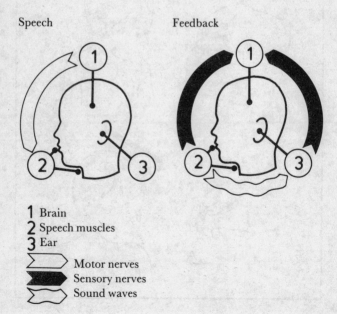

1 Brain
2 Speech muscles
3 Ear

⬡ Motor nerves
⬡ Sensory nerves
⬡ Sound waves

sounds of speech

Speaking English involves mastering over 40 speech sounds, or phonemes. Children gain this skill in two ways. First, they learn to babble, and so find out how to make a wide variety of sounds. Second, adult responses to their babbling teach them to select for use the sounds they hear most often.

Not all children learn phonemes in the same order. But phonemes do tend to appear in a pattern. Children usually say easily pronounced phonemes such as 'a' before harder ones like 's'. But the frequency with which people around them utter certain sounds also affects the learning sequence.

A typical order for the emergence of sounds is described here. By eight weeks the child utters 'a' and some other vowel sounds. By 16 weeks he mouths 'm' as well as 'b', 'g', 'k', 'p'. By 32 weeks he masters 't', 'd', 'w'. But only later will he get his tongue around 's', 'f', 'h', 'r', 'th'. Some sounds give trouble for considerable time – it may take three years to learn all 20 vowel sounds. The phonemic system is usually well established when a child is aged five to seven years.

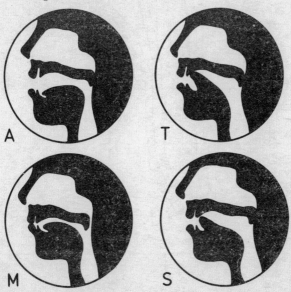

A   T

M   S

speech development

Rates of vocabulary growth vary with a child's aptitude,
parents, presence or absence of brothers and sisters, and
general living patterns.

Speech development usually starts with vocalized vowels at
about seven weeks. By 16 weeks a child utters some consonants,
and produces syllables by 20 weeks. The first meaningful word
appears at 44–48 weeks. By one year he says two or three

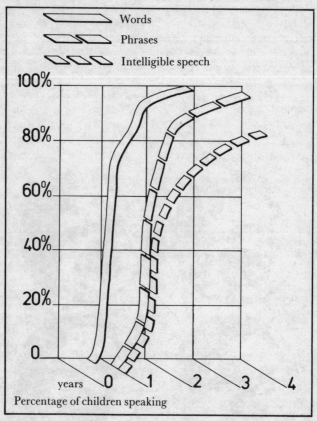

Words

Phrases

Intelligible speech

years

Percentage of children speaking

words, and by 21–24 months is using two-word phrases. By three years he talks incessantly.

Included here are two graphs showing speech development in tested groups of normal children. The first shows the percentage of children uttering words, phrases, and intelligible speech by different ages. The second shows the average number of words understood at ages up to six.

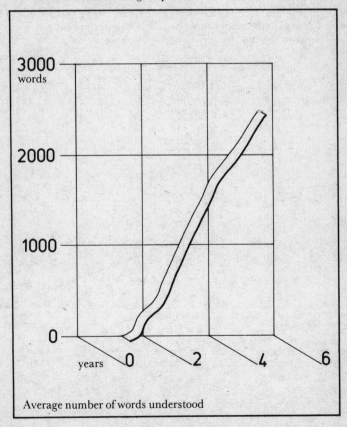

Average number of words understood

mental development

Some typical stages in a child's mental development are described here and overleaf.

Birth to 2 years The child manipulates objects in a trial and error fashion. May use observation of cause and effect to solve some simple, practical problems by action.

6 months Recognizes familiar faces, and may perceive differences between some shapes.

1 year Says first words. Defines some common objects by use.

2 years Understands simple language. Knows the difference between 'one' and 'many'. Gives own first name.

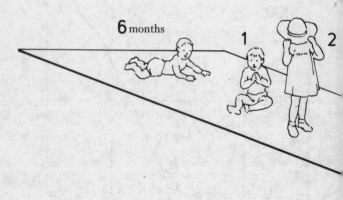

2 to 4 years Imagination is developing. Uses signs and symbols (words) to stand for absent objects and events but often confuses the sign or symbol with the thing signified or symbolized. Believes that changing an object's shape also alters its size, weight, and volume.

2½ years Understands more words than speaks. Knows own sex.

3 years Knows own age in years. Gaining accurate visual judgment of depth. Knows the difference between 'big' and 'small'.

4 years Speaks fully intelligibly and uses many words. Knows 'yesterday', 'today', and 'tomorrow'. Understands 'heavier', 'higher', and 'longer'. In attempting to reason, often confuses cause and effect.

4 to 7 years Throughout this period, intelligent behaviour is largely limited to actions. Intuitive thought is based on incomplete perceptions.

5 years Perceives relative sizes of objects well by now. Counts up to 15 bricks. May be learning to read. Can write some letters.

mental development (continued)

5 to 8 years Intersensory perception is developing rapidly.
6 years May be learning to write joined-up letters. Can say the days of the week. Counts up to 30 by rote. Knows 'right' and 'left'.
7 years Tells the time from a clock. Knows own birthday. Realizes that changing an object's shape need not mean changing the amount of the substance.

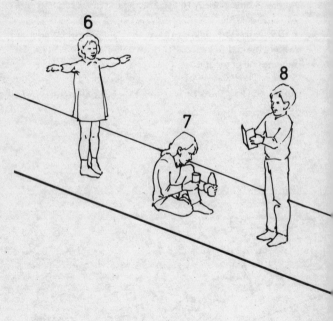

8 years Now reasons well about data he can see and touch. Enjoys reading children's books with more text than pictures. Solves simple mathematical problems.

8 to 11 years During these years children learn to group objects in classes and series. Hence concepts of space, time, and number, and realization of an ordered material world first fully emerge.

9 years Developing an abstract response to the concept of weight.

10 years Mental problem solving improves as the child draws conclusions from less concrete situations than before.

11 years Begins to reason logically about statements instead of just about concrete objects and events. Perception of physical volume is well developed by now.

12 years Historical time sense is developing. Now well able to formulate hypotheses and theories, make assumptions, and draw conclusions. Ability to reason increases through the teens.

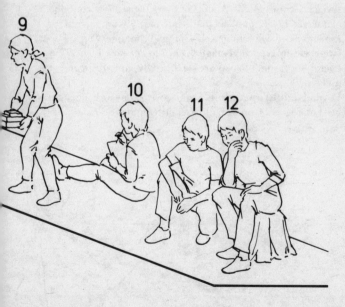

conceptual development

According to theories evolved by Swiss psychologist Jean Piaget, a child's intellectual development passes through these stages.

Sensorimotor stage From birth to 2 years. Intelligence is empirical and largely non-verbal. Muscles and senses help children deal with external objects and events. They experiment with objects and graft new experience on to old. They grasp that objects persist out of sight and touch. They start symbolizing – representing by words and gestures.

Pre-operational stage From 2 to 7 years. Children use words for perceived objects and inner feelings, and experimentally manipulate them in the mind as they physically handled objects earlier. They act by trial and error, intuition, and experience. The idea of conservation of amount and number is not yet understood. In the test shown below, a child under seven watching equal amounts of water poured into containers of unequal height may say that a tall, narrow container (**1**) receives more water than a short, broad container (**2**).

Concrete-operational stage From 7 to 12 years. Logical operations begin. Objects are classified by similarities and differences.

Formal (adult) operations From 12 years onward. Thought is used more flexibly in order to handle hypothetical issues.

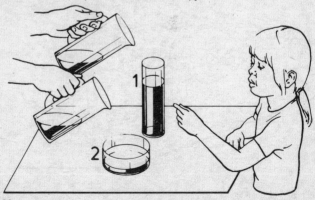

how children learn

At age two a child given a form-board puzzle tries to force a block into the hole opposite irrespective of their shapes. At 2½ years, if the block does not fit one hole the child tries to push it into another. By age three the child matches shapes by eye before placing a block in a hole.

Tests such as the one just described suggest that a child's early steps in learning are based on simple trial and error association. The puzzle is a stimulus evoking a response of effort pleasurably rewarded by solving the puzzle. Thus effort and reward become associated in the child's brain, and next time the puzzle is presented he will complete it faster. By age three he solves some problems in the mind – a process facilitated by language.

Some psychologists discount cognition ('the act of knowing') and consider that, throughout life, learning consists of mental habits formed by stimulus-response relationships.

play and development

Play is vital to a child's mental and physical development. It is one of his principal means of learning – through which he first masters basic skills, begins to express himself, and learns to get along with others.

Four broad types of play can be distinguished – active physical play, manipulative play, creative and imaginative play, and social play. Obviously some activities can be included in more than one category. The relative importance of different types of play varies with a child's age.

1) Active physical play This begins in the womb and continues all through childhood. Involving the larger motor muscles, it teaches control, coordination, and balance, and leads ultimately to all kinds of adventure and sporting activities.

2) Manipulative play This teaches the control of the finer motor muscles, particularly those in the hands. It begins soon after birth as a baby learns to grasp, lift, and squeeze, and leads eventually to mastery of skills like feeding, dressing, drawing, and writing.

3) Imaginative and creative play This type of play is especially significant as it teaches self-awareness, encourages development of imaginative powers, and allows the safe working out of emotions such as fear and aggression. Imaginative play becomes most important when the child has mastered the basic skills that enable him to express himself.

4) Social play This is an essential part of a child's emotional development. By playing first alongside other children and later with them, a child learns about cooperation, communication, and sharing. Social play thus helps him to build satisfactory relationships with others, and eventually to take up his role in the community.

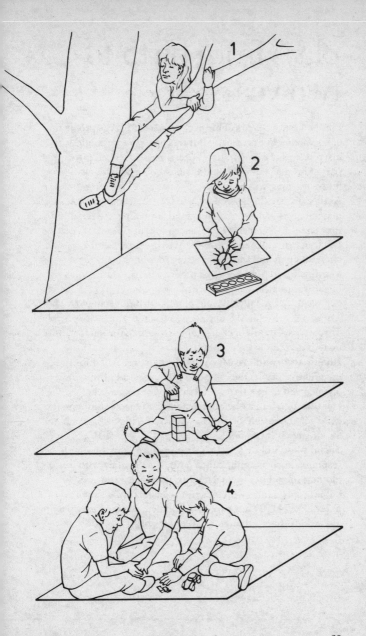

play: from birth to two years

For the first two years of life, a child spends a large proportion of his waking hours at play. But this play is never aimless, nor just a means of filling in time – it is an essential and integral part of his development, and the basis on which much of his future learning will be built.

Active physical play A baby's first form of active physical play involves kicking, reaching, and stretching. An older baby may enjoy a 'bouncer' (**1**). Wheeled toys are popular when children can walk, and climbing activities are useful for strengthening limbs and increasing muscular control.

Manipulative play For most babies, clutching an adult's finger is the earliest experience of manipulative play. A rattle (**2**), beads, a squeaky toy, and blocks, encourage an older child to grasp, lift, and build, and so help teach fine muscle control. Turning pages and scribbling are useful preparation for future imaginative and creative play.

Imaginative and creative play Among the earliest forms of imaginative play is the imitation of sounds and expressions, often copied from a parent. Picture books (**3**) and the identification and association of familiar objects stimulate the child's imagination. Simple day-to-day events provide a basis for 'acting out' situations.

Social play A baby's first social play consists of the simple responses such as smiling that result from contact with his mother; sometimes this sociability extends to strangers. Older babies enjoy games with person-to-person contact such as pat-a-cake (**4**). By age two, most toddlers start to enjoy playing alongside others – though not yet with them.

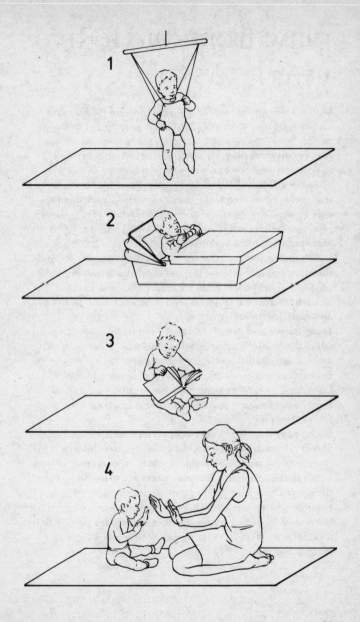

71

play: from two to five years

Between the ages of two and five play continues to be a vital and integral part of learning. Experiences gained at this time provide a basis from which learning in school can develop.

Active physical play This type of play increases in importance as the child devotes more of his time to outdoor activities and learns to run, jump, skip, hop, and climb. A tricycle (**1**) or scooter are favourite toys, and a paddling pool may be popular (although supervision is vital). Play on larger pieces of equipment such as a slide or swing is also enjoyed.

Manipulative play At this stage, activities that challenge a child's increasing dexterity such as building, jigsaws (**2**), and throwing and catching are very popular. Water and sand play are fun and help teach basic scientific principles. Using 'household equipment' increases a child's manipulative skills and exercises the imagination.

Imaginative and creative play A child starts to get the most out of this kind of play when he has mastered basic manipulative skills. Modelling and drawing (**3**) are two important expressions of creativity, and dressing up can add an extra dimension to dramatic play. Some children may now begin to appreciate a musical instrument as a means of self-expression.

Social play At first toddlers will play alongside each other, or play contentedly on the edge of a group of older children. This 'parallel' play is gradually superseded by 'cooperative' play in which the child actually includes others in his activities. From the age of about four, simple board and card games (**4**) are popular, and an older child may be happy to join a younger one in his play. Elaborate group activities such as 'tea parties' have a valuable social function as well as being a major form of imaginative play.

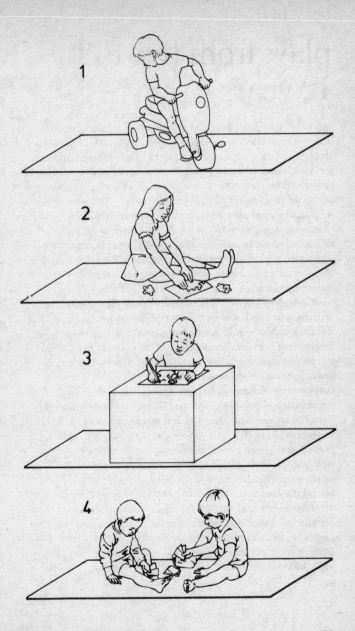

1

2

3

4

play: from five to 12 years

After the age of five the role of playthings as instruments of learning gradually becomes less important. Play for school-age children is more significant as a means of recreation, balancing the education and developmental demands of school. Another change at this time is the development of long-term hobbies and interests from simpler play activities.

Active physical play This continues in a variety of forms, ranging from simple outdoor pursuits like tree-climbing to organized sporting activities that appeal to a child's growing competitive spirit. A variety of equipment is available for active play, ranging from ropes (**1**) and hoops to scooters, bicycles, roller skates, and skateboards.

Manipulative play A child's rapidly developing manipulative skills may be applied to an almost endless range of activities in this period. Model making, embroidery (**2**), and gardening are examples of popular pastimes that may help establish lifelong interests. Particular favourites among 'playthings' for this age group are science and magic sets.

Imaginative and creative play This is now at its most significant and contributes to the process of concept learning. Creative art and craft activities and literary pursuits (**3**) have widespread appeal. Many children may also enjoy dramatic play in 'acting out' games or with puppets. Elaborate equipment such as a train set can also be a useful basis for imaginative play.

Social play After starting school a child becomes increasingly involved with others and starts to enjoy sharing his favourite activities and pastimes. More complex card games and board games (**4**) encourage shared play, but most children seem automatically to seek each other out for group activities like a walk, bicycle ride, or ball game.

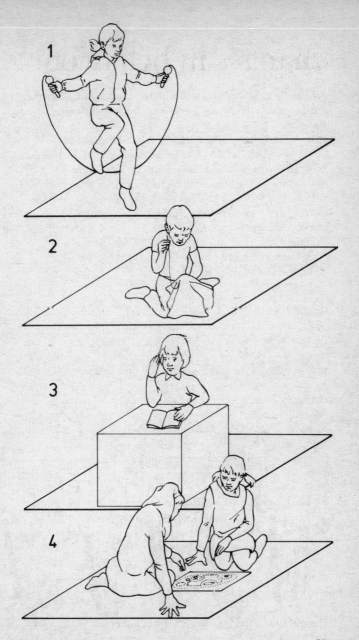

changes in behaviour

Sometimes a child gets on well with those around him. At other times he seems at odds with everyone. Psychologists have shown that, through childhood, phases when a child seems in balance with his world alternate with phases when he is unhappy and difficult. A child's personality pendulum swings between equilibrium and disequilibrium so regularly that psychologists have compiled timetables indicating when each swing is likely to occur. Behaviour fluctuating from 'focal' (eg clinging to the mother) to 'peripheral' (eg expansive and exploratory) creates another rhythm. Growth usually strikes a balance, yielding a stable, socially well-adjusted adult.
This diagram shows typical swings in behaviour during childhood and adolescence.

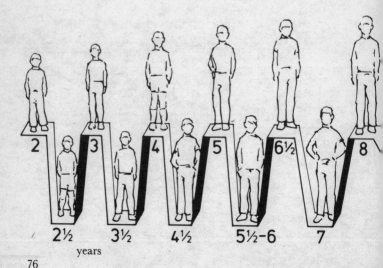

2   3   4   5   6½   8

2½   3½   4½   5½-6   7

years

2 years: well balanced
2½ years: unstable
3 years: fairly well balanced
3½ years: ingoing; unstable
4 years: lively; outgoing
4½ years: 'neurotic'
5 years: well balanced
5½–6 years: unstable; difficult
6½ years: again better balanced
7 years: withdrawn; moody
8 years: lively; outgoing
9 years: self-contained; withdrawn
10 years: well balanced; friendly
11 years: unstable
12 years: fairly well balanced
13 years: withdrawn; pessimistic
14 years: expansive; outgoing
15 years: 'neurotic'
16 years: well balanced

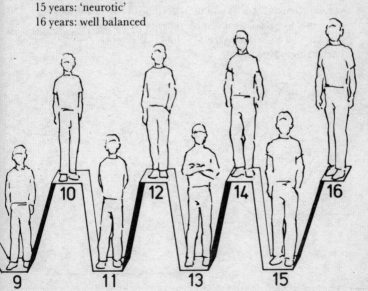

social development

Here we pick out some of the most important stages in a child's social and emotional development.

Up to 18 months By three months a child recognizes his mother (**1**). By eight months he is shy with strangers. By one year he is developing a deeper relationship with his father (**2**). Close, continuous physical and emotional contact with one person in this period is vital for developing a stable personality in adulthood.

18 months to 5 years At first, children closely identify with their parents, copying household actions (**3**). Parents discourage overdependency and outbursts of aggression. At two a child cannot yet join in games with others, but at three he does so (**4**) and shows affection for younger brothers and sisters. Speech increasingly helps the promotion of new social relationships.

5 to 12 years A five-year-old has a best friend (**5**), but group games and sports gain in importance (**6**). He seeks to identify with his contemporaries and to conform with his own school, class, and friends. Less under his parents' influence than formerly, he questions parental values that he once unthinkingly accepted.

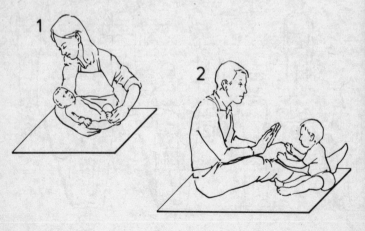

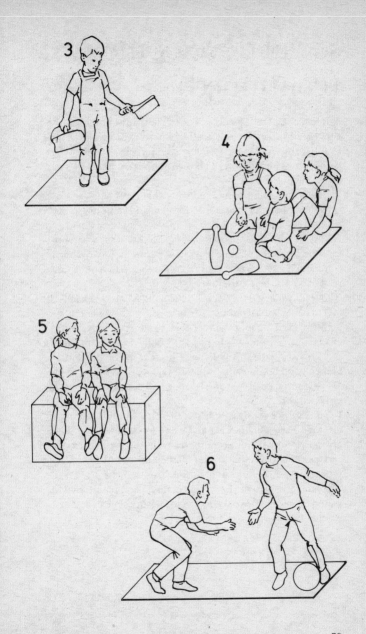

social development (continued)

Adolescence During adolescence a child must mature emotionally as well as physically. Instead of being looked after by others he will soon have to care for himself – and then perhaps also for a family of his own. This is exciting but it can be frightening too.

Interests and abilities may suddenly change. A boy who was small and physically weak may develop and shine on the sports field. Academic ability may rush ahead, or suddenly halt.

In their teens, young people no longer feel that their parents must be respected or obeyed without question. Quarrelling is common; the teenager is testing his parents to find out if he really accepts their attitudes.

Above all, adolescence is a time when the opposite sex must be met in a new way. Traditionally boys and girls do not think highly of each other in the years before puberty. This now changes. A girl who was happy and confident in her pre-teen years may become shy with boys, feel that she is unacceptable to them, and become miserable. Boys, too, need support. There are new social customs to be learned and new sexual needs to be coped with.

In adolescence young people test themselves. Only in this way can they learn who they are and what they will become. They are not yet sure if they are extroverted or shy, lighthearted or serious. Will their abilities and temperament draw them to practical work, a profession, business, or the arts?

The late teens sees the formation of moral and political views; young people conceive the sort of ideal world in which they would like to live.

Shown here and overleaf are some aspects of behaviour typical of the transition period from childhood to adulthood.

1 Before the changes and turmoils of adolescence the pre-teen child is characteristically happy and self-confident.

2 Teenagers' exploration of their own opinions and identity may lead to family rows as parental standards are challenged.

3 Teenagers also challenge school authority. In this way they test their strength and show that they will soon be adults.

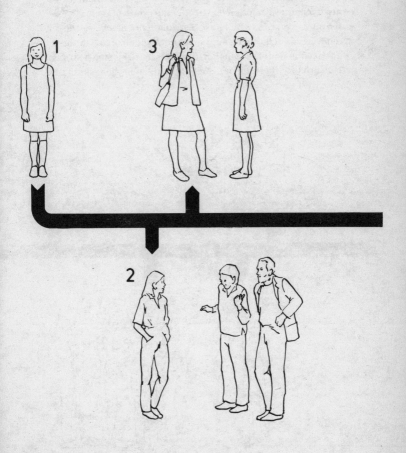

social development (continued)

4 Growing up can be frightening. Teenagers go through periods of lethargy and depression, wishing that changes were not so rapid.

5 When their friends seem to be developing faster than they are, teenagers can often feel deeply uncertain of themselves.

6 Young teenagers often have a strong sense of togetherness. They need each other's support, and dress alike to win this.

7 Mixed in with the rebellion of adolescence is often a strong concern for others and a need to help them in the tasks of life.

8 Teenagers want to know if forbidden things are really dangerous and shocking. Many try drink, smoking, and drugs.
9 Through dating, boys and girls meet each other on a more serious level. It is an essential part of getting to know the opposite sex.
10 Emerging from the trials of adolescence, the young adult seeks to make the world a better place for everyone.

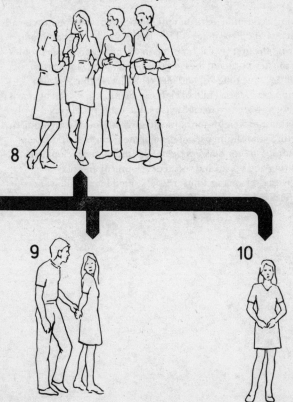

8

9

10

Section 4
AGE PROFILES

Introduction

This final section describes milestones of development typically reached at different ages. The extraordinary progress made during the first year is reflected in the inclusion of age profiles for the newborn and for ages one month, three months, six months, nine months, and one year. Development is also summarized for a child of eighteen months, and then at yearly intervals from two to eight years. Each age profile gives typical heights and weights for boys and girls, a general developmental picture, and summaries of development under four different headings: motor development, eye and hand development, hearing and voice, and social development and play.

As with previous sections, readers should make allowances for quite considerable normal variations from one child to another.

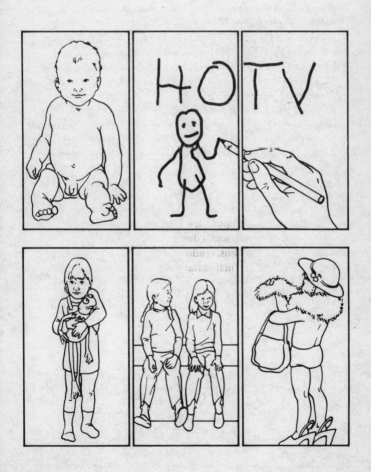

newborn

A newborn baby depends on others for almost every need. With his large head, tiny legs, soft bones, largely 'unwired' nervous system, and flabby muscles, he appears unlikely ever to achieve an independent life. Yet at least he breathes, feeds, excretes waste, and cries when hungry, and his brain is richer in promise than that of any other infant animal.

Motor development When placed face down, he lies with knees drawn up, arms bent across the chest, and head turned sideways (**1**). When held face down in the air with body horizontal, his head and limbs hang down. Walking, stepping, Moro, asymmetric tonic, and crossed extension reflexes are present (see pp. 28–30).

Eye and hand development Pupils respond to light. If suddenly dazzled by bright light, he shuts his eyes. If held erect he opens his eyes. For the first few days only, the doll's eye reflex causes his eyes to lag is he is swung in a horizontal arc (**2**). After the first week, he turns towards diffused light.

Boy
Length: 19.9in (50.5cm)
Weight: 7.5lb (3.40kg)

Girl
Length: 19.8in (50.3cm)
Weight: 7.4lb (3.35kg)

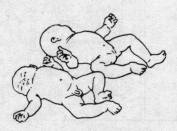

Hearing and voice Sudden sound produces blinking. He is visibly startled by sudden, loud sounds. He 'freezes' in the presence of steady, soft sounds. He cries energetically (**3**), but stops in the presence of a fairly loud, steady adult voice. His eyes may turn towards the source of a steady sound (but his head does not).

Social development and play Rooting (**4**) and sucking reflexes are present (see p. 28).

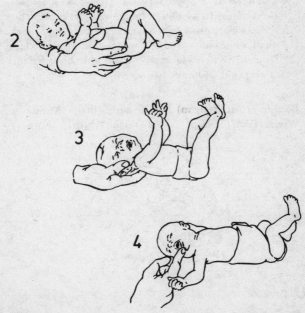

one month

The month-old baby cannot yet hold up his head, let alone sit up, crawl, or talk. He cannot even pick up an object or smile responsively. Yet his body has made tremendous progress in the first four weeks. Billions of nerve fibres effecting countless new interconnections produce much improved muscle tone, breathing, swallowing, and temperature control.

Motor development When placed face down, he lies with limbs bent, elbows out from the body, and buttocks quite high. When held face down horizontally, he keeps his head in line with his body. When lying on his back he adopts the position illustrated (**1**). He makes big, jerky movements. He stretches his limbs, fanning out his toes and fingers. He rests with his hands shut and his thumbs turned in. When his body is lifted, his head flops. When pulled to sit, he momentarily holds his head upright. When held in a standing position, he presses his feet down and adopts a walking attitude.

Eye and hand development He turns towards a source of light, and stares at a window or bright wall. His eyes briefly follow a moving, nearby light from a small flashlamp. He gazes at a small, white ball moved 6–10in (15–25cm) from his face (**2**). He alertly watches his mother's face when being fed by her. By six weeks old, he blinks defensively.

Boy
Length: 21.2in (53.8cm)
Weight: 8.6lb (3.90kg)

Girl
Length: 21.0in (53.3cm)
Weight: 8.51lb (3.86kg)

Hearing and voice A sudden noise may cause stiffening, blinking, quivering, stretching, and crying. A repeated, quiet, nearby sound causes 'freezing'. His eyes and head may turn towards a source of sound. A soothing voice stops him whimpering. He cries in hunger and discomfort. He gurgles if contented (**3**).

Social development and play Much of his time is spent sleeping. He grasps a finger that is placed in his hand (**4**). He ceases crying if picked up and talked to. He may turn to look at the face of a nearby speaker. He is responsively aware of bathing. By six weeks old he smiles socially and makes responsive sounds.

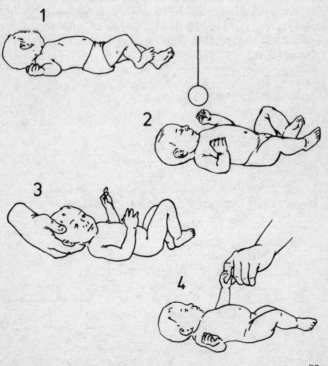

three months

At three months a baby eyes his immediate world alertly and begins to respond in a lively way. Laid face down, he struggles futilely: on his back he brings his hands above his chest. He is becoming aware of the feel of his fingers and some objects.

Motor development When placed on his stomach, he uses his forearms as props to lift his head and chest. When held face down horizontally, he raises his head and extends his hips and shoulders. Now lies on his back face upward (**1**), kicks and waves his arms, and brings his hands together above his body. There is little head lag when he is pulled to sit.

Eye and hand development He moves his head to gaze around, and briefly fixes his eyes on small objects less than 1ft (30cm) away. He alertly watches any nearby face. He watches his own hands clasping and unclasping, and in finger play. He briefly holds a rattle (**2**). He tries to focus on a small ball approaching his face. He is visibly excited by the arrival of a feeding bottle.

Boy
Length: 23.8in (60.4cm)
Weight: 12.6lb (5.55kg)

Girl
Length: 23.4in (59.4cm)
Weight: 12.4lb (5.46kg)

Hearing and voice He turns his head towards the hidden source of a nearby, intriguing sound. He is excited by the sound of a running tap, footsteps, or an approaching voice. He is quieted, unless screaming, by his mother's voice. He is distressed by loud, sudden noises. He vocalizes happily when pleased, and cries in annoyance or discomfort. He licks or sucks his lips when he hears food being prepared (**3**).

Social development and play He gazes unblinkingly at the face of a person feeding him. Baths and feeding evoke coos, smiles, and excited gestures. He enjoys being bathed and cared for. He responds happily to sympathetic handling, including tickling (**4**).

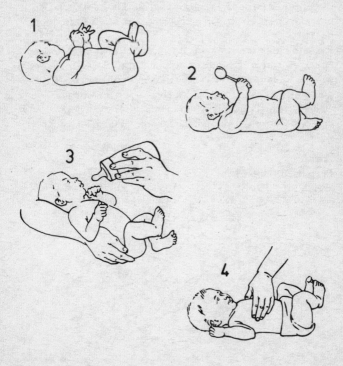

six months

Now learning the meaning of people's gestures and expressions, he reacts with two-syllabled and other sounds. His improved grasp encourages continual handling, mouthing, and banging which help him learn about objects within his reach. He still cannot sit or stand unaided but has begun to master parts of these operations.

Motor development If laid on his stomach, he extends his elbows to lift his head and chest. Lying on his back, he lifts his head to look at his feet (**1**). He lifts his legs and grabs his feet. He kicks vigorously. He rolls over. He holds his arms up to be lifted, and he pulls himself to sit if his hands are grasped. If supported he sits with his back straight and his head erect. He can briefly sit unaided. When lowered quickly, he exhibits the secondary response known as the 'downward parachute' (see p. 31).

Eye and hand development If someone attracts his attention, he eagerly moves his head and eyes in all directions. He focuses without squinting. He focuses on nearby, small objects and puts both hands out to grasp (**2**). He grasps a toy with his whole hand and passes it to his other hand. He watches dropped toys until they land, but ignores toys that land out of sight.

Boy
Length: 26.1in (66.3cm)
Weight: 16.7lb (7.58kg)

Girl
Length: 25.7in (65.3cm)
Weight: 16.0lb (7.26kg)

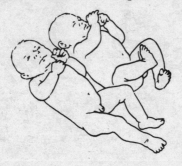

Hearing and voice He makes tuneful, sing-song, vowel and two-syllabled sounds ('goo', 'adah', 'a-a'). Hearing his mother's voice across a room, he turns at once towards the sound. He turns towards a very quiet sound from a nearby ear-level source. He responds to varying emotional sounds in his mother's voice. He screams if annoyed, and playfully squeals and chuckles (**3**).

Social development and play He uses both hands to reach out for and grab small toys. He brings everything to his mouth (**4**). He shakes and watches a rattle. He passes objects from hand to hand. He watches his own feet moving, and pats a bottle when fed. He is delighted if actively played with. By about seven months, he is shy or anxious with strangers.

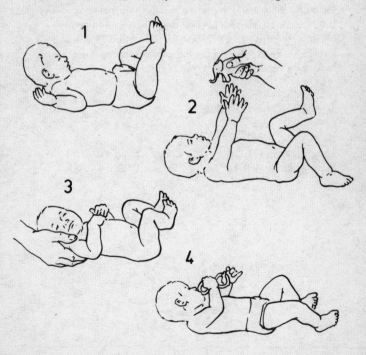

nine months

He has now mastered sitting up, and may even pull himself to
stand by holding on to the bars of his crib. Now, too, he can
begin to roll or crawl along. Fingers are controlled with
precision. He imitates simple actions, joins in some simple
games, and babbles fluently.

Motor development He can sit alone on the floor for up to 15
minutes, and is able to keep his balance while bending forward
to grasp a toy (**1**). While stretching forward to a toy, he can
turn sideways to look. He rolls or wriggles along on the floor
and tries to crawl. He pulls himself to stand and briefly remains
standing. He is extremely lively in his bath and crib.

Eye and hand development He watches nearby people or
animals for several minutes. He handles objects with interest.
He puts out one hand to grasp a toy, but stares at strange toys
before doing so. He uses his first finger to poke and point at
objects. He grips string or a biscuit between his thumb and
forefinger (**2**). He drops a toy but cannot put one down. He
looks for a toy that has fallen out of sight.

Boy
Length: 28.0in (71.1cm)
Weight: 20.0lb (9.07kg)

Girl
Length: 27.6in (70.1cm)
Weight: 19.2lb (8.70kg)

Hearing and voice He is fascinated by ordinary sounds. He understands 'no-no' and 'bye-bye'. He cannot yet localize sound produced directly above and behind him (**3**). He babbles loudly and repetitively ('ma-ma', 'da-da', etc). He shouts for attention. He makes 'friendly' and 'annoyed' sounds at other people. He copies a cough and playful vocal sounds made by adults.

Social development and play When feeding, he uses both hands to grasp a cup or bottle. He can hold, bite, and chew a biscuit. He hides his face against a familiar adult in the presence of strangers. When annoyed, he protests and stiffens his body. He holds a bell in one hand and rings it (**4**). He offers a toy to an adult but still cannot release it. He clasps hands and plays peek-a-boo in imitation of an adult. He retrieves a toy he has watched being partly or wholly hidden under a cover, or cannot discover it and cries.

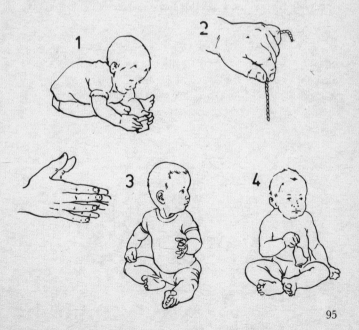

one year

Rates of growth and development are slowing. But agile crawling now gives real mobility, and the one-year-old can nearly stand and walk unaided. He repeatedly lets an object fall, and handles several objects one by one. He loves to imitate actions, speaks his first words, enjoys an audience, and shows jealousy, sympathy, and other emotions.

Motor development He can now rise from lying to sitting, and sits well for a long time. He crawls or shuffles quickly (**1**), and can perhaps crawl upstairs. He grasps furniture to pull himself up to stand, to lower himself, and to walk sideways. He walks forward, possibly unaided. He briefly stands unaided.

Eye and hand development He gazes at moving people, animals, and vehicles out of doors. He recognizes known people approaching 20ft (6.1m) away. He begins to notice pictures. He takes crumbs precisely between his thumb and the tip of his forefinger. He may favour the use of one hand. He clicks cubes together (**2**). He deliberately drops and throws toys, watching them fall. He can find a ball that has rolled out of sight.

Boy
Length: 29.6in (75.2cm)
Weight: 22.2lb (10.06kg)

Girl
Length: 29.2in (74.1cm)
Weight: 21.5lb (9.75kg)

Hearing and voice He turns when called by name. He soon ignores the sound of a hidden rattle after locating it. He understands some words in context. He understands simple commands accompanied by gestures. When requested, he hands to an adult objects such as a cup or spoon (**3**). He converses loudly in jargon. He copies playfully made vocal sounds, and repeats some words.

Social development and play He uses a cup almost unaided (**4**), and holds but cannot use a spoon. He bangs a spoon in a cup. He offers arms and feet for dressing. He rings a bell with assurance. He enjoys working sound-making toys. He soon finds toys that he has watched being hidden. Copying an adult, he inserts wooden blocks into a cup and removes them. He enjoys playing pat-a-cake. He waves 'bye-bye'. He shows affection to known adults and seeks their constant company.

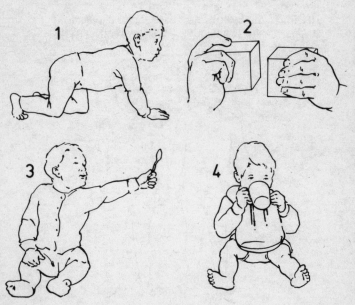

eighteen months

Immensely active, the eighteen-month-old child manipulates his body like a brash young driver trying out an automobile. Feet and arms somewhat apart, he runs about, exploring corners and clambering upstairs. He stops and starts but cannot turn corners easily or properly coordinate hands and feet. But he lugs big toys and even furniture around, learning what different places are. Lacking wrist control, he plays ball with movements of the whole arm. His world is one of here and now. His use of words is very limited. Self-willed, he takes but cannot give; and, unable to see other children as people like himself, he cannot share their play.

Boy
Height: 32.2in (81.8cm)
Weight: 25.2lb (11.43kg)

Girl
Height: 31.8in (80.8cm)
Weight: 24.5lb (11.11kg)

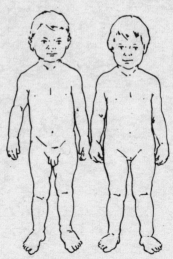

Motor development He kneels upright, unsupported (**1**). He squats to reach a toy (**2**) and stands up using hands as aids. He enjoys pulling and pushing boxes and wheeled toys around (**3**). He walks easily, with controlled starting and stopping, and feet fairly close together (**4**). He no longer needs to stretch his arms to keep balance when walking. He can run, but stares at the ground just ahead (**5**), and stops for obstacles. He likes clutching a big teddy bear or doll while walking. He walks upstairs if his hand is held, and comes downstairs crawling backward or bumping forward on his buttocks. He seats himself by backing or slipping sideways into a child's low chair, but climbs head-first into a big chair before he turns and sits.

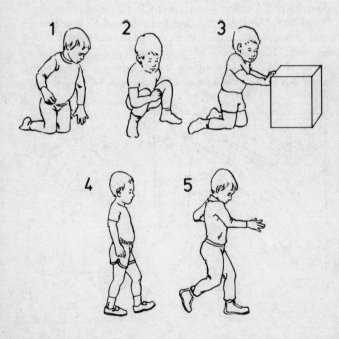

eighteen months (continued)

Eye and hand development He points to intriguing objects in the distance. He is absorbed by picture books, turns groups of pages, and points to brightly coloured illustrations. He is becoming noticeably right-handed or left-handed. Using a precise pincer grip, he swiftly picks up small objects such as beads. He grips the middle of a pencil in his palm and scribbles with it (**1**). He piles three cubes to build a tower after first being shown how (**2**).

Hearing and voice He pays attention when spoken to. He obeys requests to pass familiar named items to an adult, and also understands and performs simple tasks like shutting a door. He points to hair, shoes, etc (**3**). In play, he jabbers continually. He says 6–20 words and knows many more than that. When spoken to, he repeats the last word of a short sentence. He urgently vocalizes and points to any object that he wants. He likes nursery rhymes and attempts to say them with an adult. He tries singing.

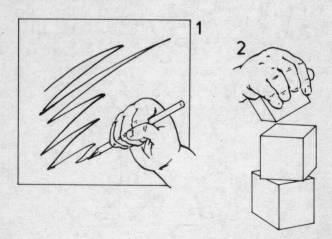

Social development and play He conveys food to his mouth
by means of a spoon (**4**). He drinks from a cup, spilling little.
He may control his bowels but not his bladder. He fidgets and
makes agitated sounds when urgently in need of the toilet. He
removes his own hat, socks, and shoes but usually cannot put
them on. He tries to open doors while energetically probing his
environment. He plays alone on the floor with toys. He likes
putting small articles into containers, and then taking them out
again. He remembers where familiar household objects are
kept. He copies everyday actions such as sweeping the floor
and reading. He still needs much emotional support from his
mother or other familiar adult, but often resists authority.

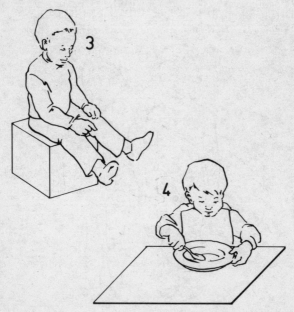

two years

No more an infant, the two-year-old gains control over bowels
and bladder, cuts his last primary teeth, and rapidly builds up
his vocabulary. Surer now upon his feet, he loves to romp,
chase, and be pursued. He seldom falls but walks with hunched
shoulders and slightly bent knees and elbows, and, as he runs,
leans forward. Rising and bending down are still done
somewhat awkwardly. Hand movements are now more varied
and assured. A twist of the wrist and he can turn a door knob.
He loves exploring objects: taking things apart; fitting things
together; pushing in and pulling out; filling and emptying. He
tests everything to hand by taste and touch. Daily chores
intrigue him and he enjoys copying them.

Boy
Height: 34.4in (87.4cm)
Weight: 27.7lb (12.56kg)

Girl
Height: 34.1in (86.6cm)
Weight: 27.1lb (12.29kg)

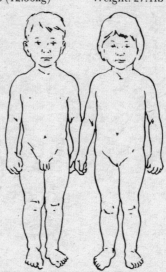

Motor development He squats steadily and stands without using his hands as props (**1**). He runs easily (**2**), controlling stops and starts, and dodging obstacles. He climbs on furniture to reach windows and door handles, and gets down unaided. He is increasingly aware of his own size compared with objects around him. He can throw a small ball forward while standing (**3**). He walks up against a big ball in an attempt to kick it (**4**). Holding a handrail or wall, he walks up and down stairs, placing both feet on each step. He steers a tricycle, sitting astride, pushing along with his feet (**5**).

two years (continued)

Eye and hand development He identifies photographs of adults well known to him (but not of himself) after one showing. He identifies miniature toys of familiar objects. He turns picture-book pages one at a time, and recognizes tiny details in the pictures. He is now definitely right-handed or left-handed. He grips a pencil near its point, between his first two fingers and thumb, makes circular to-and-fro scribbles and dots, and can copy a vertical line (**1**). He swiftly picks up tiny objects like crumbs and puts them down carefully. He can unwrap a small sweet. He uses six cubes to build a tower (**2**).

Hearing and voice He shows an interest in conversations between other people (**3**). He talks to himself continually and largely unintelligibly as he plays. He says at least 50 words and knows many more. He can say short sentences. He uses his own name to refer to himself, and asks the names of various people and things. He names (after an adult) and shows hand, mouth, shoes, etc. He participates in songs and nursery rhymes. He names and hands over familiar pictures and objects when asked to do so. He obeys simple commands, eg telling someone a meal is ready.

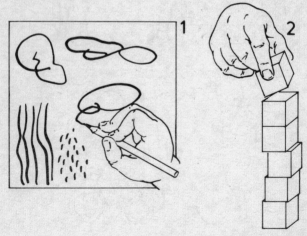

Social development and play He eats competently from a spoon and drinks from a cup. He requests food, drink, and toilet. He may be dry by day. He can put on shoes and hat (**4**). He opens doors and runs outside, oblivious of danger. He imitates his mother as she performs household chores. He demands her attention and often clings to her. He resists authority and throws tantrums if frustrated. He is fiercely possessive over toys (**5**). He does not play with other children and resents attention shown to them by his parents.

three years

The three-year-old has made great strides towards physical and psychological maturity and we glimpse in him the adult of the future. His motor mechanisms now mesh effectively: he walks erect, swings his arms in adult fashion, manoeuvres around corners, and manages stairs with ease. He is also toilet trained. Hand-eye coordination is good enough for him to draw a recognizable copy of some simple shapes. Increasing interest in words and numbers marches hand in hand with a growth of simple, verbal logic – comparing one object with another, for example. Willingness to please, to share in play and wait his turn are major pointers to the psychological progress he has made.

Boy
Height: 37.9in (96.3cm)
Weight: 32.2lb (14.61kg)

Girl
Height: 37.7in (95.8cm)
Weight: 31.8lb (14.43kg)

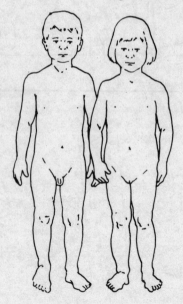

Motor development He sits on a chair, ankles crossed. He stands briefly on one leg (**1**), and can stand and walk on tiptoe. He runs and hauls and shoves big toys around obstacles. He walks forward, sideways or backward, pulling big toys. He kicks a ball hard (**2**), and catches a big ball between outstretched arms. He places one foot on each step when walking upstairs, but both feet on each step when walking down. He may jump off the bottom step. He nimbly mounts children's furniture, and pedals and steers a tricycle (**3**). He is now well aware of his own size and movements in relation to objects around him.

three years (continued)

Eye and hand development He readily picks up crumbs, with one eye covered. He cuts paper with scissors (**1**), and can build a nine-brick tower and a three-brick bridge (**2**). He controls a pencil well between his thumb and first two fingers; copies a circle and the letters HTV; draws a man, showing the head and maybe two other parts of the body (**3**). He may name colours and match three primary colours. He paints colour wash all over paper, and makes and names 'pictures'. He matches up to seven letters with test letters 10ft (3m) away.

Hearing and voice He loves hearing favourite stories (**4**). He cooperates in a hearing test by carrying out the required actions. He speaks with modulated pitch and volume. He says many intelligible words, with childish mispronunciations and mangled grammar. He uses plurals and personal pronouns correctly. He gives his own name, sex, and maybe age. He talks to himself about actions during play (**5**). He can briefly say what he is doing now and can describe past experiences. He asks countless questions starting 'what', 'where', and 'who'. He can repeat some nursery rhymes. He may be able to count to 10 but is unlikely to understand quantities greater than three.

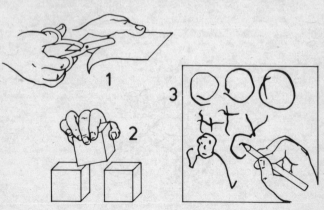

Social development and play He now uses a spoon and a fork at the table (**6**). He washes and dries his hands with help. He pulls pants up and down and can put on or take off some clothes with simple fastenings. He may now be dry by day and night. He is affectionate and less rebellious. He helps to shop, garden, etc, and tries to tidy his own toys. He plays games of make-believe, featuring imaginary people and things. He plays with other children, and shares toys and sweets (**7**). He is affectionate towards his sisters and brothers. He begins to grasp differences between past, present, and future, and no longer insists on the instant gratification of his desires.

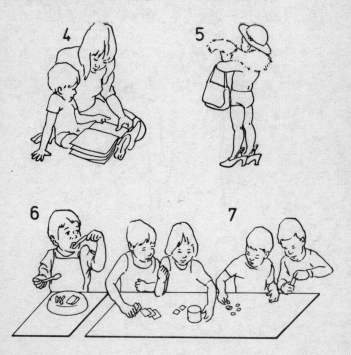

four years

Exuberant of mind and body, the four-year-old breaks through
constraints that held the three-year-old in check. Well
controlled motor muscles help him energetically climb, jump,
hop, skip, and ride a tricycle. But he is also becoming good at
tasks demanding careful hand-eye control, for instance sawing,
lacing shoes, and cutting along a line with scissors. Boastful,
bossy, and a smart aleck, he talks incessantly, trying out new
words – inventing some, and often using adult terms
incongruously out of proper context. Word play reflects the
darting movements of his thoughts, which spawn inventive
games and drawings. His mental life is blossoming.

Boy
Height: 40.7in (1.033m)
Weight: 36.4lb (16.51kg)

Girl
Height: 40.6in (1.031m)
Weight: 36.2lb (16.34kg)

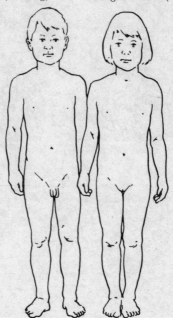

Motor development He sits on a chair with his knees crossed. He can stand, walk, and run on tiptoe. Keeping his legs straight, he can bend at the waist in order to pick up objects from the floor (**1**). He can climb trees and ladders. He is able to turn sharp corners when running. He walks or runs both upstairs and downstairs, placing only one foot on each step. He can kick, catch, throw, and bounce a ball, and strike it with a bat (**2**). He hops on his favoured foot and can balance on it for 3–5 seconds (**3**). He can make sharp turns on a tricycle.

four years
(continued)

Eye and hand development He names and matches colours.
He matches seven test-card letters with specimens 10ft (3m)
away. With one eye covered, he readily picks up and replaces
crumbs or other small objects. He can thread beads, (**1**), but
still cannot thread a needle. He builds a tower 10 cubes high
(**2**). When shown how, he arranges six cubes to build three
steps. Also when shown how, he presses his thumb against each
of his fingers in turn. He grasps a pencil maturely; he copies a
cross and the letters HOTV; he draws a man, showing head
and legs plus probably arms and trunk (**3**).

Hearing and voice He can talk intelligibly, using correct
grammar and few childish mispronunciations. He can give his
own name in full as well as his address and age. He perpetually
asks questions starting 'why', 'when', 'how'. He asks what
different words mean. He loves hearing and telling long tales,

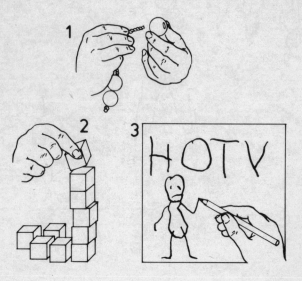

often mixing up fantasy and fact. He counts to 20 by rote, and counts actual objects up to five. He likes jokes (**4**). He accurately says or sings a few nursery rhymes.

Social development and play He handles a fork and a spoon well. He washes and dries his hands capably, and can clean his teeth (**5**). He can dress and undress except for managing difficult fastenings. Independence is shown by answering back. He is developing a sense of humour. He plays theatrical games involving dressing up. He plays complex floor games (**6**). He is less tidy than at age three. He builds things outdoors. He argues with other children, but needs their companionship and learns to take turns. He is concerned for younger brothers and sisters, and is sympathetic towards distressed playmates. He understands differences between past, present, and future.

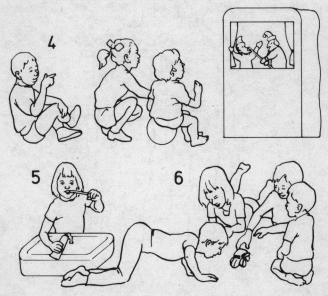

five years

Scatterbrained four develops into maturer five, whose mind works more precisely – less ruled by the mouth, as it were. He is more self-critical, and inclined to finish some project he has started. Well balanced and unflappable, the five-year-old has gained a clearer concept of himself and his role in the family and in a somewhat broader environment. He can now cope with most daily personal duties and some household tasks, and is ready for the wider world of school. But coordination of hand, eye, and brain are still developing and he is unlikely to be ready yet to learn to read and write with ease.

Boy
Height: 43.8in (1.113m)
Weight: 42.8lb (19.41kg)

Girl
Height: 43.2in (1.097m)
Weight: 41.4lb (18.87kg)

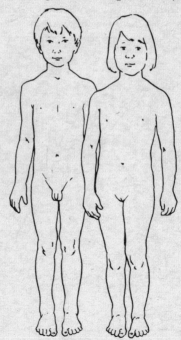

Motor development He can touch his toes while keeping his legs straight. He can stand on one foot for 8–10 seconds, and can hop 2–3yds (2–3m) forward on either foot. He skips on alternate feet, runs on his toes (**1**), and moves to music. He can walk along a thin line marked on the ground. He climbs (**2**), digs, slides, and swings. He plays ball games quite well (**3**).

five years (continued)

Eye and hand development He can match 10–12 colours. He can thread a needle and sew stitches. He can build 3–4 steps from cubes. He copies a square – and later also a triangle. He copies the letters ACHLOTUVXY, and will write some letters unprompted. He draws a man with trunk, head, arms, legs, and features (**1**); also a house with a roof, windows, door, and chimney. He colours pictures carefully. He counts the fingers of one hand.

Hearing and voice He speaks fluently and correctly but may confuse the sounds 'f', 's', and 'th'. He sings or says jingles and rhymes and likes riddles and jokes. He enjoys hearing stories and later enacts them with friends (**2**). He can quote his full name, age, birthday, and address. He explains the meaning of concrete nouns by usage and often asks what various abstract words mean.

Social development and play He uses a knife and fork well (**3**). He dresses and undresses himself. He is increasingly independent and sensible, but rather untidy. He chooses his own friends and invents involved make-believe games in which he shows a sense of fair play. He is becoming aware of clock time. He comforts distressed playmates and protects pets and young children.

3

six years

Lively, expansive, eager to try out something new, the six-year-old has an insatiable appetite for fresh experiences. But he must succeed in everything he tackles; win every game he plays; have the most of anything that's going. Otherwise there will be tears and tantrums. Six is a demanding, stubborn, and unruly age. By six years old the first adult tooth is pushing through. At school the child takes early steps along the paths that lead to an ability to read, write, and use numbers. But what he learns must be firmly based on things that he can see and do. He cannot reason in an abstract adult way.

Boy
Height: 46.3in (1.176m)
Weight: 48.3lb (21.90kg)

Girl
Height: 45.6in (1.158m)
Weight: 46.5lb (21.09kg)

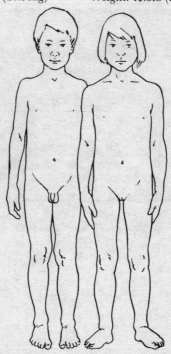

Motor development He jumps over a rope 10in (25cm) high. He hops 1–3 times on one foot so that it nudges a toy brick along. He trots around a sizeable open space such as a playground. Without a rope, he skips 12 or more times. With a rope, he manages three or more skips.

Eye and hand development He accurately copies a square and neatly copies a ladder. He attempts to copy a diamond. He draws a triangle more precisely than when aged five. He can say in two cases how one object differs from another that in some way resembles it.

Hearing and voice He can repeat accurately a sentence containing 16 syllables. He uses at least three sentences to describe a test picture. He names and recognizes at least 20 capital letters. In a verbal test he can say how one object resembles another.

Social development and play He can now be expected to behave reasonably well at table, and can cut his own meat with a knife and fork. He can tie his own shoelaces.

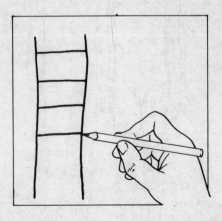

seven years

Physical and mental progress march ahead. But broadening the mind's horizons predominates over physical activity. Many a seven-year-old prefers to watch instead of do. He reads and watches television, and often likes to do so on his own partly because he feels at odds with everyone around him. Moodiness is frequent. Spells of intensive learning alternate with spasms of forgetfulness. He loves drawing and other tasks requiring precise hand-eye coordination. But he tends to overreach himself, and attempts tasks that he becomes too tired to finish.

Boy
Height: 48.9in (1.242m)
Weight: 54.1lb (24.53kg)

Girl
Height: 48.1in (1.222m)
Weight: 52.2lb (23.68kg)

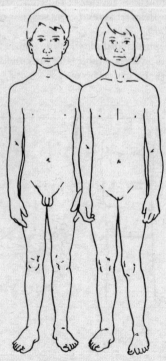

Motor development He can jump off the bottom four steps of a staircase. He can ride a two-wheeled bicycle, but not very far. He hops four times on one foot, so that it nudges a toy brick along. He can skip 12 or more times with a rope.

Eye and hand development He writes 24–26 letters. He draws a diamond neatly, and can draw a window (a cross inscribed in a square) fairly accurately. He draws a man with originality, eg clothed, side-face, seated.

Hearing and voice He can use at least four sentences to describe a test picture. He correctly answers six questions from a comprehension test list. He says in three cases how one object resembles a similar object, and also in three cases how one object differs from another that in some way resembles it.

Play and social development He has a special friend at school. Given some help, he can set a table. He brushes his own hair regularly. He can dress and undress unaided, managing fastenings well.

eight years

The eight-year-old actively explores his environment, believes no task is too hard to tackle, forms new friendships, and is concerned over people's opinions. His vocabulary is enriched by many adjectives because he now appreciates the qualities of objects and actions. But judgements involving generalizations and abstractions remain beyond him. Between now and his

Boy
Height: 51.2in (1.300m)
Weight: 60.1lb (27.27kg)

Girl
Height: 50.4in (1.280m)
Weight: 58.1lb (26.43kg)

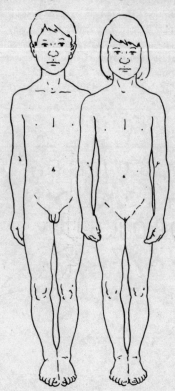

teens, the child stands somewhat on a plateau. He has a new, maturer independence of adults, and even at eight foreshadows the kind of adult he will become. But full brain development, adult stature, and sexual maturity lie well ahead.

Motor development Skips freely out of doors at least 20 times. Rides a bicycle unaided with competence in any open space considered safe.

Eye and hand development Draws a house embellished with a fair amount of detail.

Hearing and voice In four cases can say how one object differs from another that in some way resembles it. He understands and tells the time in hours, half hours, and quarter hours.

Play and social development He can set a table for everyday use, with no help at all.

Index

A SELECTED LIST OF NON-FICTION TITLES AVAILABLE FROM CORGI BOOKS

WHILE EVERY EFFORT IS MADE TO KEEP PRICES LOW, IT IS SOME-TIMES NECESSARY TO INCREASE PRICES AT SHORT NOTICE. CORGI BOOKS RESERVE THE RIGHT TO SHOW AND CHARGE NEW RETAIL PRICES ON COVERS WHICH MAY DIFFER FROM THOSE ADVERTISED IN THE TEXT OR ELSEWHERE.

THE PRICES SHOWN BELOW WERE CORRECT AT THE TIME OF GOING TO PRESS (MAY '86)

All these books are available at your bookshop or newsagent, or can be ordered direct from the publisher. Just tick the titles you want and fill in the form below.

CORGI BOOKS, Cash Sales Department, P.O Box 11, Falmouth, Cornwall.

Please send cheque or postal order, no currency.

Please allow cost of book(s) plus the following for postage and packing:

U.K. CUSTOMERS – Allow 55p for the first book, 22p for the second book and 14p for each additional book ordered, to a maximum charge of £1.75.

B.F.P.O. & EIRE – Allow 55p for the first book, 22p for the second book plus 14p per copy for the next seven books, thereafter 8p per book.

OVERSEAS CUSTOMERS – Allow £1.00 for the first book and 25p per copy for each additional book.

NAME (Block letters) ....

ADDRESS ....

....